A Lick of Loose Threads

Jenna Plewes

A toast to those who lit their lives from candle ends

First published 2023 by The Hedgehog Poetry Press

Published in the UK by
The Hedgehog Poetry Press
Coppack House, 5
Churchill Avenue
Clevedon
BS21 6QW

www.hedgehogpress.co.uk

ISBN: 978-1-913499-99-0

Copyright © Jenna Plewes 2023

The right of Jenna Plewes to be identified as the author of this work has been asserted in accordance with the Copyright, Designs and Patents Act 1988.

All rights reserved. No part of this publication may be reproduced, stored in or introduced into a retrieval system, or transmitted in any form, or by any means (electronic, mechanical, photocopying, recording or otherwise) without prior written permissions of the publisher. Any person who does any unauthorised act in relation to this publication may be liable for criminal prosecution and civil claims for damages,

9 8 7 6 5 4 3 2 1

A CIP Catalogue record for this book is available from the British Library.

1

Through Potholes and Mud

A palimpsest of lives
sealed in soil

beaded strings of pawprints,
pinpricks of claws

threaded through bramble
and blackthorn scrub

on the narrow path
trodden and re-trodden

intricately plaited ropes
of cycle treads

looping and over-lapping
sinuous as snakes

on a quilt of boot prints
stitched into mud

Scuffed and sodden trackways
turning and returning

grinding ever deeper
into torn and tender earth

So many busy, careless feet,
so many wounds

2

Tearing and Mending

Low light silvers each strand
circle soldered to circle
hung with water drops

a web stretched
seedhead to seedhead
across a muddy path

a flimsy inconvenience
easily brushed aside
without a thought

a lick of loose threads
sticking to skin
wiped off, forgotten

torn fabric
mended, re-patterned
held again in place.

3

A Toast to those who lit their lives from candle ends

Doris, whose button box spilled beads and silver buckles
whose smile lit up her tiny attic room
who taught me nonsense rhymes and fairy tales
for whom Companion spelled Beholden
and a quiet loneliness I only understood too late

teenage May, who nursed two maiden aunts,
an uncle, then another aunt, who washed them
when they died, tidied them and closed their eyes
who stayed at home while others found careers
and moved away, whose unassuming gentleness
found love at last

Kate, who hoisted her man from bed to wheelchair
wheelchair to commode, trimmed his beard, wiped drool
from his mouth, filled feeders with seeds, wheeled him to
watch the birds, hoarded the joy of unexpected holidays
each snatched hour in the sun

Joy, sixteen and still at school, who thought she was just
getting fat, whose baby lay on the palm of the midwife's hand
but never learned to hold a cup or spoon, who fought like a
mother cat for all the help he needed, had two more strapping
sons and filled her house with industry and hope

Roy, locked up for life at twenty-one, who still has dreams
and cares about his friends, who studies, learns about the world
and what it means, whose heart has conquered bitterness
with love

some days I'm plodding through the quagmire of my life and
see them squelching on ahead of me, smiling at a blink of sun
stopping to smell honeysuckle in the hedge, searching the sky
for larks. I hear their voices telling me 'It could be worse'
and though this makes me want to scream; I know they're right.

4

Traces

The hostel hummed with voices all day long
and sirens often woke her in the night
she lugged the metal teapots, stirred the stew
read to the children when they couldn't sleep
sat with those who couldn't find the words
to say what made them cut, or swallow pills.

She never told them of the man she loved
who died at Ypres with all her plans and dreams
or why she chose the grimy tenements
and left behind the peaceful hills she loved.

After she died, I found among her things
Mother's Day cards sent to 'my special mum'
and in a bottom drawer her MBE.

5

Rest-home

The smell of lunch lingers in the sitting room
they doze in orthopaedic chairs, the TV blares.
On the screen a couple wander hand-in-hand
beside a lake, kiss under a willow tree
music soars and swoops like parakeets
a black horse gallops on a beach, meercats talk.
Emely slumps sideways, her mouth open
the tea in her feeding cup's cold; there are crumbs
on her chin. Her pop-socks wrinkle round her ankles
veins vine her legs, a button's missing on her blouse.
Robert shouts, heaves himself up, his table tumbles
he subsides, muttering. Two girls bring a wheelchair
chat to each other as they push him out.
Upstairs a bell rings, rings again, keeps on ringing.
It's visiting time but no-one comes on a Monday.
Emely wakes, gropes for her feeding cup
it falls, a dribble of weak tea soaks into the carpet.

6

An Eye in the Squint

Do you remember doors nailed shut and marked for death? You were six that first time. Do you remember the plague beast slinking away, stepping outside again, going to school? You learned your letters with the nuns, did you think you'd join them in the abbey, then change your mind?

I lose you now among the narrow lanes, a small child on your hip, another on the way, hurrying home to bake and brew and sew. Was it the plague that took your man and all your little ones?

You were so young to seal yourself away, hear your funeral prayers, feel dust kiss your hands and head. Your visions ripped away the life you knew, revealed another road lit by a blaze of love. Through the long days and years, the world came to your cell for words of comfort and advice, to hear '*all will be well, all manner of things will be well*'

I hold the little book you wrote, slim enough to fit a pocket, powerful enough to echo off the walls of seven centuries, pure and sweet as birdsong after rain.

Dame Julian of Norwich 1343 – 1416 was a mediaeval anchoress who wrote the Revelations of Divine Love. The Squint is an aperture cut in the wall of the church through which an anchorite could see the altar and watch the Mass being performed.

7

Washing of Feet, Maundy Thursday Service

Stepping from sensible shoes
toes shrinking from cold stone
she waits her turn

ice cold sea
skirt tucked in her nickers
sun splintering shallows

feet cradled in huge hands
warm water on cracked skin, blotted with gentleness
pricking of unexpected tears

salt-sticky skin
sandpapered dry
gritty school sandals, shifting shingle

just once a year
the feel of fingers
pressing love in every thirsty pore.

8

Pilgrim Feet

have borne
his weight all day
gnarled bony feet
burnt brown as bark.

Barefoot, the soles
felt every pebble
every puff of dust
prickle of dry grass
blister of sun-cracked clay.

Now as he knees, they rest
cupped like hands in prayer
holding his weary earthbound
supplications.

on seeing Madonna of the Rosary 1607 Caravaggio

9

Inpatient

Desert fatigues
lie neatly folded
in the hospital locker
boots crusted with sand
pushed out of sight.

No longer anchored
by commands
buttressed by mates
he listens to the squeak
of trolley wheels
disembodied voices.

Dog tired
gripping a dead phone
he wades uncharted waters
unfamiliar currents
hidden depths

waiting for orders.

10

Platoon

The machine on the 7th floor
dispenses hot drinks
plastic cups go in the pedal bin.

From up here you look down on trees
Lowry figures at a bus stop
a keyboard of car roofs.

In a patch of sunlight
six lads sprawl on a bench
beside a boy in a wheelchair.
He strokes his empty trouser leg
lights up a cigarette, draws deep
sends a thread of smoke into the darkening sky
then stubs it out
before they wheel him back inside.

As they walk away
one calls
keep on it, mate, back soon, see you.

11

Battleground

New terrain, new tactics
grab-handles in the shower
non-slip seat, sterile surfaces

see the set of his shoulders
the look in his eyes

green beret, correctly angled
medals: pinned right breast pocket

notice how erect he stands
one trouser-leg rolled to the thigh
one to the knee, the metal legs

as he sets out each day
to navigate nightmares,
the hidden tripwires of the mind.

12

Remembrance Sunday

As if togetherness
were tangible
they come in tidy lines
booted and beribboned
poppies pinned in place

among the khaki uniforms
a woman dressed in black
walking with a child
three men in wheelchairs
line abreast

the bands play
rank on rank follow
through streets
hung with multi-coloured flags

the church bell tolls
silence gathers them in
the choir's white surplices
shift in the breeze

sunlight reads the names
engraved in stone

two girls in running shorts
a man with a guide dog
stand with the rest

where each must lie alone
the sound of bugles
echoing
from cairn
to cairn
of piled up memories.

13

Zero Hours Contract

His thoughts are far away,
long fingers press the iron
down on the darkness
sealing it in.

Only the smell of scorching cloth
drags his hands away, his mind
back to the quiet room
the laundry basket

the table covered with a folded sheet
a single bed, one kitchen chair
rail with a shirt, trousers
cotton jacket.

Each evening he peels off the day
washes off the grime, wrings
out the residue,
irons a clean shirt

each morning he buttons himself
into a clean linen day
smooth, polished
pressed.

14

Crane

8am
he
climbs
rung
after
rung
from
earth
into
air

slips into a box
small as a cone
on a lodgepole pine
places his hands
on a keyboard

stretches out an arm, longer than any arm should be
lowers
      block
            after building block
                    in place

below him

hard hats cluster like ant's eggs
yellow beetles scurry to-and-fro
sirens and flashing lights needle
through forests of skyscrapers

alone up there with gulls and sky
fingers hovering over buttons
he balances a world on his shoulders

then
comes
rung
by rung
down
to earth

joins the tide of commuters
swirling among towering
slabs of concrete and glass
to eat a meal, sleep in a bed

while
up there
a small
red light
challenges
the stars.

15

The Lady in the Big House

No-one would bend and peak under the brim - that would be unthinkable
like undressing her in public

whenever she ventured out, she wore a wide brimmed hat, or a bonnet
clustering her face

her winter coat had an outsized hood trimmed with rabbit fur, and when it rained
she tied a sou'wester under her chin.

A hat to keep my hair neat on a windy day. Something suitable for the weather - to keep off the sun, or the rain.

A carefully constructed camouflage to slip from shadow to shadow in the jungle out there
with its snakes and poison darts.

When she died, we found the hatboxes – exotic hats with sweeping brims, a rainbow of bonnets, all nested in tissue

we never saw her face, the colour of her eyes, whether they crinkled when she smiled. We only knew the hats.

16

A New Year

She takes down the 2020 calendar, opens the new one at January and transcribes birthdays and anniversaries into the coming year, a ritual that becomes more and more necessary now her memory's getting unreliable.
    She sits at the kitchen table in the winter sun and reads through the past year – plans she'd made and pencilled in, celebrations, meetings, reunions: ones she'd looked forward to, some she'd dreaded, all cancelled or postponed indefinitely. There are funerals in there too. Quiet, lonely ones with a handful of relatives and without the comfort of companionship. That's what's been missing all these months, the chat, the hugs, the reminiscing – being together, being where things happen, having things to look forward to.
    She checks she's remembered everyone, then hangs up the calendar where she can see it easily. The January picture's a painting of a green hillside, a tractor climbing to the skyline, a blizzard of gulls, blue sky overhead.

> A cloudless sky
> seagulls following the plough
> furrows ready for seed

17

Playing with Fire

She teases it with a long match till it wriggles free, claws its way
up the paper twists she's pushed into hollows in her dome of twigs

she feeds it slivers of shavings, dry grass, cardboard, then branches, sees it
grow hungry, gorging armfuls of prunings, old cardigans, a feather duster

motheaten carpet, broken spade handles, old bamboo canes. It feels good,
letting go of everything, all her regrets, inhibitions hoarded a lifetime.

The wind rises, driving the fire in a frenzy. Pine needles spit, sparks singe her hair,
flames lick her face. Smoke sears her throat. The heat frightens her.

It's a mistake, wanting too much. She leans on her spade, waits till the fire
smoulders, rakes in the rim of twigs and trash, leaving the ground blackened
and bare.

No-one will come; the phone won't ring. Her muscles ache as she climbs the
stairs. From
her bedroom window she sees a night breeze stir the last few shreds to life,
then all is dark.

Stepping Into Her Shoes

From the bed, she watches him struggle
the man who can change a wheel
by the side of a road in the rain
who chairs the parish council
with good humoured efficiency
a man confronted with an ironing board.

The height finally adjusted to his satisfaction
he inspects the jumble of crumpled laundry
rummages for the white shirt he'll need
in the morning, dumps it on the board
pulls at the tangled sleeves, lifts the iron
hauling on the twisted flex, sighs.

She clamps her mouth shut, her fingers
itch to demonstrate:

start with the inside of the collar, then a sleeve, pull it straight, run the iron down, turn the sleeve and do the other side; don't forget the cuff; now the other sleeve. Next the fronts, push the prow of the iron between the buttons, over the button holes. Press the front carefully, this is what shows under a jacket. It's more important than the sleeves. Now the long sweep of the back, ease each shoulder over the nub of the board and smooth the seam.

Put it on a hanger while it's still warm and don't forget to do up the top button so the shirt doesn't crease.

She dozes fitfully, listens to the thump
of the iron, hiss of steam, rasp of the flex,
hears the familiar intake of breath, the dry cough.
If she opened her eyes, she'd see the thick grey hair
the set of his jaw, deep lines each side of his mouth
the eyes of a small boy alone at the school gates
struggling with a shoelace.

19

Body-blow

No-one hears the heartwood crack
the willow slowly fall apart. Darkness
curtains it, rain washes the wounds.

Sunlight circles a shadow dance, plays
with an upright branch, a fringe of leaves
the rest lie twisted, splayed in the dirt.

But roots hold, heart beats, sap runs,
buds form, break into leaf, stems will
grow back, climb towards the light.

Shaped and reshaped by weathering,
ordinary will become extraordinary
will have a broken beauty of its own.

Someone one day will sense another's
heartbreak, the stumbling will to live,
will put their own load down to listen.

A Meeting of Minds

A maple leaf sticks to his sleeping bag
a lick of gold he puts between the pages
of the paperback he'll finish tonight.
Tomorrow the girl will find him on his patch
they'll talk about the books they read, exchange
a few. She studying philosophy, lives in a flat,
comes in by bus. Monday 8.45am they'll squat
on the pavement with takeout coffees, playing
with ideas, he'll be nodding and listening
to what she has to say, sharing what he loved,
still loves; before his life went off the rails.

21

Transit

The city's arteries are clotted with decay, capillaries gangrenous
slimed with algae; shadowy hideaways for hunted and forgotten ones.

Wharves and warehouses are lost in bramble and buddleia, watery snickets
home to lilies, purple loosestrife, moorhens, pike, herons, water rats.

No barges, clang of metal on metal, clatter of hobnail boots, now
shopping trolleys, sofa cushions, broken bikes clog the waterways.

In Gas Street Basin narrowboats moor beside restaurants and bars
sunlight blinds the thousand eyes of tower-blocks, trams like silvery eels

glide through shopping mall and plaza. Feet pound treadmills, taxis
circle like foraging bees, a homeless girl begs in an underpass.

22

Home was barefoot in damp grass
wrapped in silence like silk
a tang of salt and chamomile
and something indefinable
found there and nowhere else

a past wrapped in birthday paper
hidden under the floorboards of a house
reduced to rubble, a coffin filled with dust.

Home's now the smell of cooking oil, chips
the squeal of brakes and traffic lights
music, voices, running feet, umbrellas
cloudy skies and endless rain. Home
is a room furnished with scraps of
woollen comfort, a door with a key.

23

Making a go of things

Today's dissolving in the mush of memory
the café's blinds are down, a takeaway cup
floats in a pool of light from the co-op.

Becca is packing up, only two Big Issues sold
she puts her big umbrella and her camping chair
behind the wheelie-bins; they'll be safe there.

This is her pitch, tea from the café, a sandwich
from the co-op, people are kind. She smiles
keeps her voice bright; but if you take the time

she'll tell you how her little brother wets the bed -
it's not his fault, he has bad dreams. The flat
is cold, it's hard to dry the sheets in winter.

Her mother's homesick, cries in the night.
And you, I ask, *are you sad too?*
She smiles, *I like it here, I have this job.*
Now tell me about you; are you ok?

24

Sasha and Me at Nursery
Sasha's new, she sat by me today.
She talks funny but I really like her;
she doesn't push or shove, take my things
without asking, I'll let her sit by me tomorrow.

We drew houses on big paper; mine had
a front door, a chimney with smoke,
a window with me looking out,
a big tree by the gate, a path and bushes.

Sasha's was all squiggly and messy;
she can't draw well, but I didn't say;
her house was wobbly, didn't even
have a roof. There were no bushes
or a path, just scribbles and lots of holes.

Tomorrow is painting day. I'll need
lots of yellow for a big sun, blue for
sky and flowers. Sasha wants blue
and yellow too, for a flag.
She wants red and black as well.
I'll let her have the fat brush,
it's best for black and red.
Her painting will be very messy;
but I won't say.

Show and Tell's my favourite thing.
I brought my train with the carriage.
Sasha brought a teeny-tiny doll,
it's hard, like a bean, shiny with
lots of colours, I really like it.
She said all the bigger ones got lost,
it's the only one left. We put it
in the carriage; that cheered her up.
She giggles like me sometimes now.

25

Mother and Son

Remember those up-and-down Devon lanes
the farm collie that snapped at our wheels
as we cycled past steep banks of primroses
fathoms of bluebells, snowdrifts of ransoms

those sea-green bottles tinged with lustre we found
in a midden, crusted with dregs of liniment, remedies
for chills and aching bones, I still have some,
stoppered with sunlight, on my windowsill.

Remember the pram chassis for trundling the canoe
to the canal, ducklings scooting like wind-up toys
moorhens chugging among the reeds
the dip and lift of our paddles, curl of green water

how the canal slid like a snake through a hole in the hill
a distant glimmer beckoning us in
we never dared that blindfold mile, the cold drip
drip of water, echoes splashing slippery walls

how easy it looked, how you begged to go on.
I stand on the bank, look at that far away glow
think of your open-hearted, roller-coaster life; wonder
what dark places you paddle now to reach the light.

26

OS map 198

She's set the alarm for 7.30; it will give her plenty of time
to get the 9.30 bus. It looks as if it will be fine tomorrow
but she'll take his golf umbrella just in case.

The sandwiches she made are in the fridge
wrapped in clingfilm; cheese and the last of the chutney
he made with the all those windfalls.

She'll take a flask of coffee, and his favourite mug
a screw-top bottle with a tot of whiskey; just in case,
pack everything in his old rucksack.

She'll wear her walking boots, the socks he gave her
last Christmas and his old scarf. She'll have the OS map
with the torn cover and the scribbles in the margin.

When she gets there, she'll remember what he said,
*don't go too close to the edge, make sure you have
the wind at your back.*

And she'll let him go. Then she'll spread out the map,
read the notes he made in the margin, and follow the path
they planned; but never found the time to take.

27

Picking Raspberries

They're like firm, pink nipples -
as she pulls berries from the stalks
her breasts remember that pull

a baby's head rooting under her shirt
fingers splayed like starfish
the snuffle of feeding.

The children say they worry about her
the garden, the creaking house
the distance from the shops.

She breast-strokes a rustling green tide
slowly down the rows, eating berries
one for the basket - one for her.

These are stubby old canes now
new ones would bear more fruit.
She planted these; they're enough.

28

Tomorrow she'll be 80

looking back, she can see
how the path zigzags,
detours
then doubles back
how tangles become
untangled, the way
straightens out again.

The air smells of apples
a curlew spools loneliness
and sorrow into the wind
a buzzard high overhead
unreels its plans.

She can see for miles
an ocean of sky
mountains, moorland
and in the distance
the breathing sea.

She longs to turn back time
wash away the scum in the seas
the filth from the land
bring back the world she knew

the buzzard's just a speck
above her now, a faint cry
carries on the breeze
She shoulders her rucksack
with its muddle
of unanswered questions
moves on.

29

With love

Snowdrops and winter jasmine
wrapped in damp kitchen roll, later
powdery catkins, bluebells in a jam-jar.

The carer finds them on the doorstep
stuffs them in the mug without a handle
brings them up with her breakfast.

When she's downstairs in her wheelchair
she places them on the windowsill beside her
watches the light circle round them

she'll see the old man with the even older collie
the woman with a toddler and twin buggy
the girl with a ponytail and bulging school bag.

On a good day she'll lift a hand as they pass,
lean towards the window till they're out of sight,
try to guess who leaves the flowers on the step.

Fingers and Thumb

the thumb began as comfort
                  suckling sleep
                  became a thinking place

the index finger stroked
                  the soft breast of an owl
                  pointed the way

the next lifted a curl in place
                  on a wedding day,
                  pressed into the future

the four's heavy with rings
                  grooved with love
                  and memories

the littlest nestles close,
                  is brave enough to
                  stretch an octave

five fingers
                  cup them to hold a promise
                  curl them over to keep it.

Acknowledgements

Thank you, Rebecca Hubbard for your workshops that inspired a number of these poems. Thank you my buddies, Kathie Gee, Sarah Leaverson and John Lawrence for your honest criticism, my friends in Cannon Poets, the Moor poets, my Inktank group without whose feedback and encouragement this collection would have been the poorer. Thank you, Jane Easton for the beautiful painting that is on the cover and Mark at Hedgehog Press for sending these poems out into the world.

www.ingramcontent.com/pod-product-compliance
Lightning Source LLC
Chambersburg PA
CBHW030313100526
44590CB00012B/627